WHY DO ANIMALS HAVE

Elizabeth Miles

www.heinemann.co.uk/library
Visit our website to find out more information about **Heinemann Library** books.

To order:
 Phone 44 (0) 1865 888066
 Send a fax to 44 (0) 1865 314091
 Visit the Heinemann Bookshop at www.heinemann.co.uk/library to browse our catalogue and order online.

First published in Great Britain by Heinemann Library, Halley Court, Jordan Hill, Oxford OX2 8EJ, a division of Reed Educational and Professional Publishing Ltd. Heinemann is a registered trademark of Reed Educational & Professional Publishing Limited.

OXFORD MELBOURNE AUCKLAND JOHANNESBURG BLANTYRE
GABORONE IBADAN PORTSMOUTH NH (USA) CHICAGO

Designed by David Oakley@Arnos Design
Originated by Dot Gradations
Printed in Hong Kong.

ISBN 0 431 15310 8
06 05 04 03 02
10 9 8 7 6 5 4 3 2 1

British Library Cataloguing in Publication Data

Miles, Elizabeth
Why do animals have eyes
1.Eye - Juvenile literature 2.Physiology - Juvenile literature
I.Title
573.8'8'1

Acknowledgements
The Publishers would like to thank the following for permission to reproduce photographs: BBC NHU/Pete Oxford p. 16; BBC NHU/Bruce Davidson p. 17; BBC NHU/David Welling p. 26; BBC NHU/Dietmar Nill p. 28; BBC NHU/G&H Denzau p. 19; BBC NHU/Steve Packham p. 21; Bruce Coleman Collection/Kim Taylor p. 22; Bruce Coleman Collection/Felix Labhardt p. 23; Bruce Coleman Collection/John Cancalosi p. 13; Bruce Coleman Collection/ Werner LayerBruce p. 10; Corbis p. 27; Corbis/Robert Pickett p. 14; digital vision pp. 8, 24, 30; NHPA/Daniel Heuclin p. 7; NHPA/Norbert Wu p. 15; NHPA/Stephen Dalton p. 9; OSF/Scott Smith p. 6; OSF/David Fox p. 18; OSF/Neil Bromhall p. 29; OSF/Sue Scott p. 20; OSF/Tom Ulrich p. 25; OSF/Adrian Bailey p. 5; OSF/Tony Tilford p. 11; Photodisc p. 4; Stone/Daniel J. Cox p. 12.

Cover photograph reproduced with permission of Oxford Scientific films/Rafi Ben-Shahar.

Our thanks to Claire Robinson, Head of Visitor Information and Education at London Zoo, for her help in the preparation of this book.

Contents

Words in bold, **like this**, are explained in the Glossary.

Why do animals have eyes?

People have eyes and so do most animals. You are using your eyes to read this book and look at the pictures. Every day, you use your eyes to see the world around you. Seeing is an important **sense**.

These meerkats are using their eyes to look out for danger. If one meerkat sees a dangerous animal, it can warn the others. They will all run and hide in a **burrow**.

Eyeballs, lids and lashes

The main part of the eye is the eyeball. A squid's eyeballs stick out from its head. It uses its eyes to look for fish and other sea animals to eat.

Like your eyes, giraffe's eyes have a top and bottom **eyelid.** They close to protect the giraffe's eyes from bright light. **Blinking** keeps eyes **moist.** The giraffe's long **eyelashes** help keep out dust and flies.

Eyes for looking forward

People and some animals have eyes that face forwards. Their eyes are at the front of their heads. This helps hunting animals to catch **prey**. A tiger can tell exactly how far away its prey is.

Owls have forward-facing eyes. They can see well enough to catch fast-moving creatures. They can snatch a moth flying through the air or a mouse running along the ground.

Looking all around

Some animals, such as deer, have eyes on the sides of their head. This means they can see see all around. A deer can look out for **predators** while it is **grazing**.

Most birds have eyes at the sides of their head. They can look around for danger, without moving their head. A woodcock's eyes are so far back that it can see behind itself.

Eyes in flight

Some birds have very sharp **eyesight** for catching **prey**. A flying hawk can spot a mouse far below on the ground. Hawks can see much better than people can.

Hawks and eagles are **birds of prey**. Unlike most birds, their eyes face slightly forwards. They can see a wide area. They can see the middle part of that area very clearly.

Underwater eyes

Fish have an eye on each side of their head. They can see to the left and the right at the same time. Fish do not need **eyelids**, because they live in water.

Some fish are called four-eyed fish because each eye has two parts. The top part points up and watches out for hungry birds in the sky. The bottom part looks down through the water, searching for food.

Night eyes

Some **nocturnal** animals have eyes that shine in the dark. Their special eyes help them to see more clearly at night. A leopard sees far better than we can in the dark.

Bush babies have very big eyes. They wake up at night to find food. Bush babies can see so well that they can jump from tree to tree in the dark.

Protected eyes

Most birds' eyes have three **eyelids**, instead of two. The third eyelid closes to shield the eye from bright light and dust. The bird can still see through this eyelid.

Camels live in sandy deserts. Camels have thick **eyelashes** and a third eyelid to protect each eye. In a **sandstorm** a camel closes its third eyelids. This stops sand from blowing into its eyes, but the camel can still see.

Tiny eyes

A scallop is an animal with a shell. It peers through the water with lots of tiny eyes. These cannot see very well, but they can spot something moving nearby. The scallop watches out for **predators**.

Most spiders have eight tiny eyes. The largest two eyes can see quite well. They can see the difference between another spider and an **insect** it can eat. The other eyes watch out for movements that might be a predator.

Thousands of eyes

Most **insects** have what look like two eyes. A dragonfly's eyes curve round its head. It can see in lots of different directions at the same time.

The dragonfly has two sets of eyes. Each set has up to 30,000 tiny **lenses**. These are six-sided and fit neatly together. Each lens sees a small part of what the dragonfly is looking at.

Bulging eyes

Some animals have eyes that bulge, or stick out. This gives them a good view. Red-eyed tree frogs have bulging eyes so they can look out for **predators**.

A chameleon's eyes bulge from its head. By **swivelling** its eyes, the chameleon can look in two directions at once. The **eyelids** are round and protect most of each eye.

Eyes on stalks

Some animal eyes stick out a long way. Slugs' eyes are on the ends of stalks. The slug can move the stalks to look over small objects, and to look around and behind.

Eyes on stalks are useful when creatures want to hide. Crabs with eyes on stalks can stay hidden in the sand, while their eyes watch for **predators**.

Living without seeing

Some animals that live in the dark cannot see, so they use other **senses** instead. Some salamanders that live in dark caves use smell and touch to find their way.

Mole rats live in **burrows** underground. It is very dark and the mole rats are nearly blind. They also use the **senses** of smell, touch and hearing to find their way.

Fact file

- Lots of animals cannot see as many colours as we can. Dogs and squirrels cannot tell the difference between reds and greens. Birds can see more shades of colours than we can.

- Giant squids have two huge eyes. Each eye is at least twice the size of your head!

- Some butterflies have markings on their wings that look like eyes. These 'false' eyes frighten **predators** away.

Long-eared owl fledglings can see in the dark.

Glossary

birds of prey birds that catch food (animals) with their feet

blinking closing the eye quickly and often

burrow underground hole or nest

eyelash a hair on the rim of the eye

eyelid covering over the eye

eyesight the ability to see

grazing eating low-growing grass or plants

insect small animal with three main parts to its body and six legs

lens part of the eye that light passes through

moist a bit wet or damp

nocturnal awake and active at night, not during the day

predators animals that hunt other animals for food

prey animals hunted as food

sandstorm strong wind that blows clouds of sand along

sense way of being aware of the world (seeing, hearing, smell, touch and taste are senses)

swivelling moving in any direction

Index

Titles in the *Why Do Animals Have* series include:

Hardback 0431 15311 6

Hardback 0431 15310 8

Hardback 0431 15326 4

Hardback 0431 15323 X

Hardback 0431 15314 0

Hardback 0431 15312 4

Hardback 0431 15322 1

Hardback 0431 15325 6

Hardback 0431 15313 2

Hardback 0431 15324 8